perfect pasta

Essential dishes for everyday cooking

Love Food ® is an imprint of Parragon Books Ltd

Parragon
Queen Street House
4 Queen Street
Bath BA1 1HE, UK

ISBN: 978-1-4075-2873-1

Printed in China

Designed by Talking Design
Cover text and introduction by Lorraine Turner

Notes for the reader
This book uses both metric and imperial measurements. Follow the same units of measurement throughout; do not mix metric with imperial. All spoon measurements are level, unless otherwise stated: teaspoons are assumed to be 5 ml and tablespoons are assumed to be 15 ml. Unless otherwise stated, milk is assumed to be semi-skimmed, eggs and individual vegetables such as potatoes are medium, and pepper is freshly ground black pepper. Recipes using raw or very lightly cooked eggs should be avoided by infants, the elderly, pregnant women, convalescents and anyone suffering from an illness. The times given are an approximate guide only.

Contents

introduction

It is tempting to think of pasta as a modern food, but its earliest use can been traced to an Etruscan tomb some 50 kilometres from Rome. The tomb dates back to around 400 BCE, and shows the Etruscans making a kind of lasagne. In those days they probably used spelt, a cereal similar to wheat, but hardier and easier to store.

We know that the ancient Romans made lasagne. By the 13th century macaroni was in widespread use in Italy, and by the 17th century pasta had spread to Europe. It is said that US President Thomas Jefferson fell in love with macaroni on a visit to Naples in the 18th century and introduced it to the people of the United States. From there it flourished even more and became a firm favourite all over the world.

Today, variations of this popular food can be found all around the globe. For example, the Chinese have perfected the use of egg noodles in stir-fries, and the Spanish use wonderfully fine, vermicelli-like noodles called 'fideos'. These are particularly delicious added to

clear soups and make them more substantial and satisfying.

Pasta is unparalleled for its versatility. It is very easy to make at home, although commercially available pasta is of such high quality that it is no longer necessary to make it yourself. It comes in a very wide range of shapes and sizes, from long noodles and rectangular sheets, to bows, spirals and shells.

Preparing and cooking pasta

It is very easy and quick to prepare and cook pasta, so this food is ideal for the novice and more experienced cook alike. It is also very handy if you are short of time. Fresh unfilled pasta needs only 3 minutes to cook, or 10 minutes if it is filled. For example, you would need to boil fresh fettucine (long noodles) in water for only 3 minutes, or fresh ravioli (filled pasta 'cushions') for 10 minutes.

If you are using dried pasta, you will need to cook it for 10–12 minutes if it is unfilled, and 15–20 minutes if it is filled.

Enticing accompaniments

Pasta is delicious served on its own, simply seasoned with salt and freshly ground black pepper and drizzled with olive oil. However, it also makes the perfect partner for a wide range of delicious and exciting sauces. Top a platter of freshly cooked spaghetti with a rich tomato and beef sauce, for example, and you have the classic Spaghetti Bolognese, or why not try omitting the beef from the tomato sauce and creating a Spaghetti Napoletana for vegetarians?

You can top your pasta with cream-based sauces, or sauces using meat, fish or vegetables, so the combinations are truly endless. Simply scatter over some freshly grated Parmesan cheese, perhaps add an accompaniment of some garlic bread warmed

in the oven, and you have an irresistible meal to tempt the most discerning palate.

Essential equipment

You don't need any special equipment to prepare and cook pasta, just a large saucepan for boiling the pasta in water, and one or two heatproof dishes for baked pasta recipes such as lasagne. A pasta ladle has 'teeth' around the edge, and is helpful for lifting drained pasta noodles onto plates, but is not essential. Likewise, a pasta machine is not essential because shop-bought pasta is so good these days, but if you prefer to make your own, you will find it very helpful for rolling out your freshly made pasta and cutting it into ribbons, noodles and a variety of decorative shapes.

The recipes in this book use a wide variety of dried pasta. However, for the more adventurous cook, follow the recipe below to make your own beautiful fresh version:

Basic Pasta Dough

Serves 3–4
200 g/7 oz strong white flour, plus extra for dusting
pinch of salt
2 eggs, lightly beaten
1 tbsp olive oil

Sift together the flour and the salt onto a work surface and make a well in the centre with your fingers. Pour the eggs and oil into the well, then, using the fingers of one hand, gradually incorporate the flour into the liquid.

Knead the dough on a lightly floured work surface until it is completely smooth. Wrap in clingfilm and leave to rest for 30 minutes before rolling out or feeding through a pasta machine. Resting makes the dough more elastic.

soups & salads

Tomato Broth
with Angel Hair Pasta

SERVES 4

500 g/1 lb 2 oz ripe tomatoes,
    peeled and halved

8 garlic cloves, peeled but left whole

1 onion, chopped

½ tsp saffron threads, lightly crushed

1 tsp sugar

1 bouquet garni

5-cm/2-inch strip thinly pared lemon
    rind

600 ml/1 pint vegetable or chicken
    stock

2 tbsp extra virgin olive oil

280 g/10 oz dried angel hair pasta

salt and pepper

Put the tomatoes, garlic cloves, onion, saffron, sugar, bouquet garni and lemon rind into a large, heavy-based saucepan. Pour in the stock and bring to the boil, then reduce the heat, cover and simmer, stirring occasionally, for 25–30 minutes, until the tomatoes have disintegrated.

Remove the pan from the heat and leave to cool slightly. Remove and discard the garlic cloves, bouquet garni and lemon rind. Ladle the tomato mixture into a food processor or blender and process to a purée.

Return the purée to the rinsed-out pan and season to taste with salt and pepper. Stir in the olive oil and bring to the boil. Add the pasta, bring back to the boil and cook for 2–4 minutes, until the pasta is tender but still firm to the bite.

Taste and adjust the seasoning, if necessary. Ladle the broth and pasta into warmed soup bowls and serve immediately.

Tortellini
in Broth

SERVES 6

3 tbsp olive oil

1 red onion, finely chopped

2 garlic cloves, finely chopped

350 g/12 oz fresh beef mince

1 tsp finely chopped fresh thyme

1 fresh rosemary sprig,
   finely chopped

1 bay leaf

1¾ litres/3 pints beef stock

2 x quantity Basic Pasta Dough
   (see page 5)

plain flour, for dusting

1 egg, lightly beaten

salt and pepper

Heat the oil in a saucepan. Add the onion and garlic and cook over a low heat, stirring occasionally, for 5 minutes, until softened but not browned. Add the beef, increase the heat to medium and cook, stirring with a wooden spoon to break up the meat, for 8–10 minutes, until evenly browned. Stir in the herbs, season with salt and pepper, add 125 ml/4 fl oz of the stock and bring to the boil. Reduce the heat, cover and simmer for 25 minutes, then remove the lid and cook until all the liquid has evaporated. Remove the pan from the heat, discard the bay leaf and leave to cool.

Roll out the pasta dough on a lightly floured surface to 2–3 mm/ 1⁄16–1⁄8 inch thick. Using a 2-cm/3⁄4-inch plain biscuit cutter, stamp out rounds. Place about ¼ teaspoon of the meat mixture in the centre of each round. Brush the edges of each round with a little beaten egg, then fold the rounds in half to make half-moons and press the edges to seal. Wrap a half-moon around the tip of your index finger until the corners meet and press together to seal. Repeat with the remaining half-moons. Place the filled tortellini on a floured tea towel and leave to dry for 30 minutes.

Bring the remaining stock to the boil in a large saucepan. Add the tortellini, bring back to the boil and cook for 3–4 minutes, until tender but still firm to the bite. Ladle the tortellini and broth into warmed soup bowls and serve immediately.

Fish Soup
with Macaroni

SERVES 6

2 tbsp olive oil

2 onions, sliced

1 garlic clove, finely chopped

1 litre/1¾ pints fish stock or water

400 g/14 oz canned chopped
   tomatoes

¼ tsp herbes de Provence

¼ tsp saffron threads

115 g/4 oz dried macaroni

18 live mussels, scrubbed and
   debearded

450 g/1 lb monkfish fillet, cut into
   chunks

225 g/8 oz raw prawns, peeled and
   deveined, tails left on

salt and pepper

Heat the olive oil in a large, heavy-based saucepan. Add the onions and garlic and cook over a low heat, stirring occasionally, for 5 minutes, or until the onions have softened.

Add the fish stock with the tomatoes and their can juices, herbs, saffron and pasta and season to taste with salt and pepper. Bring to the boil, then cover and simmer for 15 minutes.

Discard any mussels with broken shells or any that refuse to close when tapped. Add the mussels, monkfish and prawns to the pan. Re-cover the pan and simmer for a further 5–10 minutes, until the mussels have opened, the prawns have changed colour and the fish is opaque and flakes easily. Discard any mussels that remain closed. Ladle the soup into warmed bowls and serve.

Pasta &
Potato with Pesto Soup

SERVES 4

2 tbsp olive oil

3 rindless, smoked bacon rashers,
  finely chopped

25 g/1 oz butter

450 g/1 lb floury potatoes, chopped

450 g/1 lb onions, finely chopped

600 ml/1 pint chicken stock

600 ml/1 pint milk

100 g/3½ oz dried conchigliette

150 ml/5 fl oz double cream

2 tbsp chopped parsley

salt and pepper

freshly grated Parmesan cheese,
  to serve

Pesto

55 g/2 oz finely chopped fresh parsley

2 garlic cloves, crushed

55 g/2 oz pine kernels, crushed

2 tbsp chopped fresh basil leaves

55 g/2 oz freshly grated Parmesan
  cheese

150 ml/5 fl oz olive oil

white pepper, to taste

To make the pesto, put all of the ingredients in a food processor or blender and process for 2 minutes, or blend by hand using a pestle and mortar.

Heat the oil in a large saucepan and cook the bacon over a medium heat for 4 minutes. Add the butter, potatoes and onions and cook for 12 minutes, stirring constantly.

Add the stock and milk to the saucepan, bring to the boil and simmer for 10 minutes. Add the conchigliette and simmer for a further 3–4 minutes.

Blend in the cream and simmer for 5 minutes. Add the chopped parsley, salt and pepper to taste and 2 tablespoons of the pesto sauce. Transfer the soup to individual serving bowls and serve with Parmesan cheese.

Pasta Salad
with Walnuts & Dolcelatte

SERVES 4

225 g/8 oz dried farfalle

2 tbsp walnut oil

4 tbsp safflower oil

2 tbsp balsamic vinegar

280 g/10 oz mixed salad leaves

225 g/8 oz dolcelatte cheese, diced

115 g/4 oz walnuts, halved and
   toasted

salt and pepper

Bring a large, saucepan of lightly salted water to the boil. Add the pasta, bring back to the boil and cook for 8–10 minutes, or until tender but still firm to the bite. Drain and refresh in a bowl of cold water. Drain again.

Mix the walnut oil, safflower oil and vinegar together in a jug, whisking well, and season to taste with salt and pepper.

Arrange the salad leaves in a large serving bowl. Top with the pasta, cheese and walnuts. Pour the dressing over the salad, toss lightly and serve.

Pasta Salad
with Chargrilled Peppers

SERVES 4

1 red pepper

1 orange pepper

280 g/10 oz dried conchiglie

5 tbsp extra virgin olive oil

2 tbsp lemon juice

2 tbsp pesto

1 garlic clove, crushed

3 tbsp shredded fresh basil leaves

salt and pepper

Put the whole peppers on a baking sheet and place under a preheated grill, turning frequently, for 15 minutes, until charred all over. Remove with tongs and place in a bowl. Cover with crumpled kitchen paper and set aside.

Meanwhile, bring a large saucepan of lightly salted water to the boil. Add the pasta, bring back to the boil and cook for 8–10 minutes, until tender but still firm to the bite.

Combine the olive oil, lemon juice, pesto and garlic in a bowl, whisking well to mix. Drain the pasta, add it to the pesto mixture while still hot and toss well. Set aside.

When the peppers are cool enough to handle, peel off the skins, then cut open and remove the seeds. Chop the flesh coarsely and add to the pasta with the basil. Season to taste with salt and pepper and toss well. Serve at room temperature.

Rare Beef
with Pasta Salad

SERVES 4

450 g/1 lb rump or sirloin steak in
  1 piece

450 g/1 lb dried fusilli

4 tbsp olive oil

2 tbsp lime juice

2 tbsp Thai fish sauce

2 tsp clear honey

4 spring onions, sliced

1 cucumber, peeled and cut into
  2½-cm/1-inch chunks

3 tomatoes, cut into wedges

3 tsp finely chopped fresh mint

salt and pepper

Season the steak to taste with salt and pepper, then grill or pan-fry for 4 minutes on each side. Leave to rest for 5 minutes, then, using a sharp knife, slice the steak thinly across the grain and reserve until required.

Meanwhile, bring a large saucepan of lightly salted water to the boil. Add the pasta, bring back to the boil and cook for 8–10 minutes until tender but still firm to the bite. Drain thoroughly, refresh in cold water and drain again. Toss the pasta in the oil.

Mix the lime juice, fish sauce and honey together in a small saucepan and cook over a medium heat for about 2 minutes.

Add the spring onions, cucumber, tomato wedges and mint to the pan, then add the steak and mix well. Season to taste with salt.

Transfer the pasta to a large, warmed serving dish and top with the steak and salad mixture. Serve just warm or leave to cool completely.

Niçoise
Pasta Salad

SERVES 4

350 g/12 oz dried conchiglie

115 g/4 oz green beans, topped and
  tailed

50 g/1¾ oz canned anchovy fillets,
  drained

2 tbsp milk

2 small crisp lettuces

3 large beef tomatoes

4 hard-boiled eggs

225 g/8 oz canned tuna, drained

115 g/4 oz stoned black olives

salt

Vinaigrette Dressing

3 tbsp extra virgin olive oil

2 tbsp white wine vinegar

1 tsp wholegrain mustard

salt and pepper, to taste

Bring a large saucepan of lightly salted water to the boil. Add the pasta, bring back to the boil and cook for 8–10 minutes, until tender but still firm to the bite. Drain and refresh in cold water.

Bring a small saucepan of lightly salted water to the boil over a medium heat. Add the green beans and cook for 10–12 minutes, or until tender but still firm to the bite. Drain, refresh in cold water, drain again and reserve.

Put the anchovies in a shallow bowl, pour over the milk and leave to stand for 10 minutes. Meanwhile, tear the lettuces into large pieces. Blanch the tomatoes in boiling water for 1–2 minutes, then drain, peel and roughly chop the flesh. Shell the eggs and cut into quarters. Divide the tuna into large chunks.

Drain the anchovies and the pasta. Put all the salad ingredients together into a large bowl and gently mix.

To make the vinaigrette dressing, beat together all the dressing ingredients and chill in the refrigerator until required. Just before serving, pour the vinaigrette dressing over the salad.

Pasta Salad
with Melon & Prawns

SERVES 6

225 g/8 oz green fusilli

5 tbsp extra virgin olive oil

450 g/1 lb cooked prawns

1 Charentais melon

1 Galia melon

1 tbsp red wine vinegar

1 tsp Dijon mustard

pinch of caster sugar

1 tbsp chopped fresh flat-leaf parsley

1 tbsp chopped fresh basil

1 oakleaf lettuce, shredded

salt and pepper

fresh basil leaves, to garnish

Bring a large saucepan of lightly salted water to the boil. Add the pasta, bring back to the boil and cook for 8–10 minutes, until tender but still firm to the bite. Drain, toss with 1 tablespoon of the olive oil and leave to cool.

Meanwhile, peel and devein the prawns, then place them in a large bowl. Halve both the melons and scoop out the seeds with a spoon. Using a melon baller or teaspoon, scoop out balls of the flesh and add them to the prawns.

Whisk together the remaining olive oil, the vinegar, mustard, sugar, parsley and chopped basil in a small bowl. Season to taste with salt and pepper. Add the cooled pasta to the prawn and melon mixture and toss lightly to mix, then pour in the dressing and toss again. Cover with clingfilm and chill in the refrigerator for 30 minutes.

Make a bed of shredded lettuce on a serving plate. Spoon the pasta salad on top, garnish with basil leaves and serve.

meat & poultry

Spaghetti
Bolognese

SERVES 4

1 tbsp olive oil

1 onion, finely chopped

2 garlic cloves, chopped

1 carrot, chopped

1 celery stick, chopped

50 g/1¾ oz pancetta or streaky
  bacon, diced

350 g/12 oz fresh lean beef mince

400 g/14 oz canned chopped
  tomatoes

2 tsp dried oregano

125 ml/4 fl oz red wine

2 tbsp tomato purée

350 g/12 oz dried spaghetti

salt and pepper

chopped fresh parsley, to garnish

Heat the oil in a large frying pan. Add the onion and cook for 3 minutes. Add the garlic, carrot, celery and pancetta and sauté for 3–4 minutes, or until just beginning to brown.

Add the beef and cook over a high heat for another 3 minutes or until all of the meat is brown. Stir in the tomatoes and their can juices, the oregano and red wine and bring to the boil. Reduce the heat and leave to simmer for about 45 minutes.

Stir in the tomato purée and season to taste with salt and pepper.

Bring a large saucepan of lightly salted water to the boil. Add the pasta, bring back to the boil and cook for 8-10 minutes, until the pasta is tender but still firm to the bite. Drain thoroughly.

Transfer the spaghetti to a serving plate and pour over the bolognese sauce. Toss to mix well, garnish with parsley and serve hot.

Spaghetti
with alla Carbonara

SERVES 4

450 g/1 lb dried spaghetti

1 tbsp olive oil

225 g/8 oz rindless pancetta or
streaky bacon, chopped

4 eggs

5 tbsp single cream

2 tbsp freshly grated Parmesan
cheese

salt and pepper

Bring a large, saucepan of lightly salted water to the boil. Add the pasta, bring back to the boil and cook for 8–10 minutes, or until tender but still firm to the bite.

Meanwhile, heat the olive oil in a heavy-based frying pan. Add the pancetta and cook over a medium heat, stirring frequently, for 8–10 minutes.

Beat the eggs with the cream in a small bowl and season to taste with salt and pepper. Drain the pasta and return it to the pan. Tip in the contents of the frying pan, then add the egg mixture and half the Parmesan cheese. Stir well, then transfer to a warmed serving dish. Serve immediately, sprinkled with the remaining cheese.

Pepperoni
Pasta

SERVES 4

3 tbsp olive oil

1 onion, chopped

1 red pepper, deseeded and diced

1 orange pepper, deseeded and diced

800 g/1 lb 12 oz canned chopped
   tomatoes

1 tbsp sun-dried tomato purée

1 tsp paprika

225 g/8 oz pepperoni sausage, sliced

2 tbsp chopped fresh flat-leaf parsley,
   plus extra to garnish

450 g/1 lb dried penne

salt and pepper

Heat 2 tablespoons of the olive oil in a large, heavy-based frying pan. Add the onion and cook over a low heat, stirring occasionally, for 5 minutes, or until soft. Add the red and orange peppers, tomatoes and their can juices, sun-dried tomato purée and paprika and bring to the boil.

Add the pepperoni and parsley and season to taste with salt and pepper. Stir well, bring to the boil, then reduce the heat and simmer for 10–15 minutes.

Meanwhile, bring a large, saucepan of lightly salted water to the boil. Add the pasta, bring back to the boil and cook for 8–10 minutes, or until tender but still firm to the bite. Drain well and transfer to a warmed serving dish. Add the remaining olive oil and toss. Add the sauce and toss again. Sprinkle with parsley and serve immediately.

Rigatoni
with Chorizo & Mushrooms

SERVES 4

4 tbsp olive oil

1 red onion, chopped

1 garlic clove, chopped

1 celery stick, sliced

400 g/14 oz dried rigatoni

280 g/10 oz chorizo sausage, sliced

225 g/8 oz chestnut mushrooms, halved

1 tbsp chopped fresh coriander

1 tbsp lime juice

salt and pepper

Heat the oil in a frying pan. Add the onion, garlic and celery and cook over a low heat, stirring occasionally, for 5 minutes, until soft.

Meanwhile, bring a large saucepan of lightly salted water to the boil. Add the pasta, bring back to the boil and cook for 8–10 minutes, until tender but still firm to the bite.

While the pasta is cooking, add the chorizo to the frying pan and cook, stirring occasionally, for 5 minutes, until evenly browned. Add the mushrooms and cook, stirring occasionally, for a further 5 minutes. Stir in the coriander and lime juice and season to taste with salt and pepper.

Drain the pasta and return it to the pan. Add the chorizo and mushroom mixture and toss lightly. Divide between individual warmed plates and serve immediately.

Farfalle
with Gorgonzola & Ham

SERVES 4

225 ml/8 fl oz crème fraîche

225 g/8 oz chestnut mushrooms, quartered

400 g/14 oz dried farfalle

85 g/3 oz Gorgonzola cheese, crumbled

1 tbsp chopped fresh flat-leaf parsley, plus extra sprigs to garnish

175 g/6 oz cooked ham, diced

salt and pepper

Pour the crème fraîche into a saucepan, add the mushrooms and season with salt and pepper. Bring to just below the boil, then reduce the heat and simmer very gently, stirring occasionally, for 8–10 minutes, until the cream has thickened.

Meanwhile, bring a large saucepan of lightly salted water to the boil. Add the pasta, bring back to the boil and cook for 8–10 minutes, until tender but still firm to the bite.

Remove the pan of mushrooms from the heat and stir in the cheese until it has melted. Return the pan to a very low heat and stir in the parsley and ham.

Drain the pasta and add it to the sauce. Toss lightly, then divide between individual warmed plates, garnish with parsley sprigs and serve.

Tagliatelle
with Spring Lamb

SERVES 4

750 g/1 lb 10 oz boneless lean lamb in
  a single piece
6 garlic cloves, thinly sliced
6–8 fresh rosemary sprigs
125 ml/4 fl oz olive oil
400 g/14 oz dried tagliatelle
55 g/2 oz butter
175 g/6 oz button mushrooms
salt and pepper
freshly shaved pecorino cheese,
  to serve

Using a sharp knife, make small incisions all over the lamb, then insert a garlic slice and a few rosemary leaves in each incision. Heat 2 tablespoons of the oil in a large heavy-based frying pan. Add the lamb and cook over a medium heat, turning occasionally, for 25–30 minutes, until tender and cooked to your liking.

Meanwhile, chop the remaining rosemary and place in a mortar. Add the remaining oil and pound with a pestle. Season to taste with salt and pepper and set aside.

Remove the lamb from the heat, cover with foil and leave to stand. Bring a large saucepan of lightly salted water to the boil. Add the pasta, bring back to the boil and cook for 8–10 minutes, until tender but still firm to the bite.

Meanwhile, melt the butter in another saucepan. Add the mushrooms and cook over a medium–low heat, stirring occasionally, for 5–8 minutes, until tender.

Drain the pasta, return it to the pan and toss with half the rosemary oil. Uncover the lamb and cut it into slices. Divide the tagliatelle between individual warmed plates, season with pepper and top with the lamb and mushrooms. Drizzle with the remaining rosemary oil, sprinkle with the cheese and serve immediately.

Pappardelle
with Chicken & Porcini

SERVES 4

40 g/1½ oz dried porcini mushrooms

175 ml/6 fl oz hot water

800 g/1 lb 12 oz canned chopped
  tomatoes

1 fresh red chilli, deseeded and finely
  chopped

3 tbsp olive oil

350 g/12 oz skinless, boneless chicken,
  cut into thin strips

2 garlic cloves, finely chopped

350 g/12 oz dried pappardelle

salt and pepper

2 tbsp chopped fresh flat-leaf parsley,
  to garnish

Place the porcini in a small bowl, add the hot water and leave to soak for 20 minutes. Meanwhile, place the tomatoes and their can juices in a heavy-based saucepan and break them up with a wooden spoon, then stir in the chilli. Bring to the boil, reduce the heat and simmer, stirring occasionally, for 30 minutes, or until reduced by half.

Remove the mushrooms from their soaking liquid with a slotted spoon, reserving the liquid. Strain the liquid through a coffee filter paper or muslin-lined sieve into the tomatoes and simmer for a further 15 minutes.

Meanwhile, heat 2 tablespoons of the olive oil in a heavy-based frying pan. Add the chicken and cook, stirring frequently, until golden brown all over and tender. Stir in the mushrooms and garlic and cook for a further 5 minutes.

While the chicken is cooking, bring a large, saucepan of lightly salted water to the boil. Add the pasta, bring back to the boil and cook for 8–10 minutes, or until tender but still firm to the bite. Drain well, transfer to a warmed serving dish, drizzle with the remaining olive oil and toss lightly. Stir the chicken mixture into the tomato sauce, season to taste with salt and pepper and spoon on top of the pasta. Toss lightly, sprinkle with parsley and serve immediately.

Pasta
with Two Sauces

SERVES 4

250 g/9 oz dried green tagliatelle

salt

fresh basil leaves, to garnish

Tomato Sauce

2 tbsp olive oil

1 small onion, chopped

1 garlic clove, chopped

400 g/14 oz canned chopped
   tomatoes

2 tbsp chopped fresh parsley

1 tsp dried oregano

2 bay leaves

2 tbsp tomato purée

1 tsp sugar

salt and pepper

Chicken Sauce

55 g/2 oz unsalted butter

400 g/14 oz skinless, boneless
   chicken, cut into thin strips

85 g/3 oz blanched almonds

300 ml/10 fl oz double cream

salt and pepper

To make the tomato sauce, heat the oil in a saucepan over a medium heat. Add the onion and cook until translucent. Add the garlic and cook for 1 minute. Stir in the tomatoes, parsley, oregano, bay leaves, tomato purée and sugar. Season to taste with salt and pepper, bring to the boil and simmer, uncovered, for 15–20 minutes, until reduced by half. Remove the pan from the heat and discard the bay leaves.

To make the chicken sauce, melt the butter in a frying pan over a medium heat. Add the chicken and almonds and cook for 5–6 minutes, or until the chicken is cooked through.

Meanwhile, bring the cream to the boil in a small saucepan over a low heat and boil for about 10 minutes, until reduced by almost half. Pour the cream over the chicken and almonds, stir and season to taste with salt and pepper. Reserve and keep warm.

Bring a large saucepan of lightly salted water to the boil. Add the pasta, bring back to the boil and cook for 8-10 minutes, until the pasta is tender but still firm to the bite. Drain and transfer to a warmed serving dish. Spoon over the tomato sauce and arrange the chicken sauce on top. Garnish with fresh basil leaves and serve.

fish
&
seafood

Spaghetti
alla Puttanesca

SERVES 4

3 tbsp olive oil

2 garlic cloves, finely chopped

10 canned anchovy fillets, drained
and chopped

140 g/5 oz black olives, stoned and
chopped

1 tbsp capers, drained and rinsed

450 g/1 lb plum tomatoes, peeled,
deseeded and chopped

pinch of cayenne pepper

400 g/14 oz dried spaghetti

salt

2 tbsp chopped fresh parsley,
to garnish

Heat the oil in a heavy-based frying pan. Add the garlic and cook over a low heat, stirring frequently, for 2 minutes. Add the anchovies and mash them to a pulp with a fork. Add the olives, capers and tomatoes and season to taste with cayenne pepper. Cover and simmer for 25 minutes.

Meanwhile, bring a large, saucepan of lightly salted water to the boil. Add the pasta, return to the boil and cook for 8–10 minutes, or until tender but still firm to the bite. Drain well and transfer to a warmed serving dish.

Spoon the anchovy sauce into the dish and toss the pasta, using 2 large forks. Garnish with the chopped parsley, and serve immediately.

Spaghetti
with Tuna & Parsley

SERVES 6

500 g/1 lb 2 oz dried spaghetti

25 g/1 oz butter

200 g/7 oz canned tuna, drained

55 g/2 oz canned anchovies, drained

250 ml/9 fl oz olive oil

1 large bunch of fresh flat-leaf
  parsley, coarsely chopped

150 ml/5 fl oz crème fraîche

salt and pepper

Bring a large saucepan of lightly salted water to the boil. Add the pasta, bring back to the boil and cook for 8-10 minutes, until the pasta is tender but still firm to the bite. Drain the spaghetti in a colander and return to the pan. Add the butter, toss thoroughly to coat and keep warm until required.

Flake the tuna into smaller pieces using 2 forks. Place the tuna in a food processor or blender with the anchovies, oil and parsley and process until the sauce is smooth. Pour in the crème fraîche and process for a few seconds to blend. Taste the sauce and season with salt and pepper, if necessary.

Warm 6 plates. Shake the pan of spaghetti over a medium heat for a few minutes, or until it is thoroughly warmed.

Pour the sauce over the spaghetti and toss quickly, using 2 forks. Serve immediately.

Springtime
Pasta

SERVES 4

2 tbsp lemon juice

4 baby globe artichokes

7 tbsp olive oil

2 shallots, finely chopped

2 garlic cloves, finely chopped

2 tbsp chopped fresh flat-leaf parsley

2 tbsp chopped fresh mint

350 g/12 oz dried rigatoni

12 large uncooked prawns

25 g/1 oz unsalted butter

salt and pepper

Fill a bowl with cold water and add the lemon juice. Prepare the artichokes one at a time. Cut off the stems and trim away any tough outer leaves. Cut across the tops of the leaves. Slice in half lengthways and remove the central fibrous chokes, then cut lengthways into 5-mm/¼-inch thick slices. Immediately place the slices in the bowl of acidulated water to prevent discoloration.

Heat 5 tablespoons of the oil in a heavy-based frying pan. Drain the artichoke slices and pat dry with kitchen paper. Add them to the frying pan with the shallots, garlic, parsley and mint and cook over a low heat, stirring frequently, for 10–12 minutes, until tender.

Meanwhile, bring a large saucepan of lightly salted water to the boil. Add the pasta, bring back to the boil and cook for 8–10 minutes, until tender but still firm to the bite.

Peel the prawns, cut a slit along the back of each and remove and discard the dark vein. Melt the butter in a small frying pan and add the prawns. Cook, stirring occasionally, for 2–3 minutes, until they have changed colour. Season to taste with salt and pepper. Drain the pasta, tip it into a bowl. Add the remaining oil and toss well. Add the artichoke mixture and the prawns and toss again. Serve immediately.

Linguine
with Prawns & Scallops

SERVES 6

450 g/1 lb raw prawns

25 g/1 oz butter

2 shallots, finely chopped

225 ml/8 fl oz dry white vermouth

350 ml/12 fl oz water

450 g/1 lb dried linguine

2 tbsp olive oil

450 g/1 lb prepared scallops, thawed
  if frozen

2 tbsp snipped fresh chives

salt and pepper

Peel and devein the prawns, reserving the shells. Melt the butter in a heavy-based frying pan. Add the shallots and cook over a low heat, stirring occasionally, for 5 minutes, or until soft. Add the prawn shells and cook, stirring constantly, for 1 minute. Pour in the vermouth and cook, stirring, for 1 minute. Add the water, bring to the boil, then reduce the heat and simmer for 10 minutes, or until the liquid has reduced by half. Remove the frying pan from the heat.

Bring a large saucepan of lightly salted water to the boil. Add the pasta, bring back to the boil and cook for 8–10 minutes, until the pasta is tender but still firm to the bite.

Meanwhile, heat the oil in a separate heavy-based frying pan. Add the scallops and prawns and cook, stirring frequently, for 2 minutes, or until the scallops are opaque and the prawns have changed colour. Strain the prawn-shell stock into the pan. Drain the pasta, add to the pan with the chives and season to taste with salt and pepper. Toss well over a low heat for 1 minute, then serve.

Tagliatelle
in a Creamy Prawn Sauce

SERVES 4

3 tbsp olive oil

3 tbsp butter

4 garlic cloves, very finely chopped

2 tbsp finely diced red pepper

2 tbsp tomato purée

125 ml/4 fl oz dry white wine

450 g/1 lb dried tagliatelle

350 g/12 oz raw peeled prawns

125 ml/4 fl oz double cream

salt and pepper

3 tbsp chopped fresh flat-leaf parsley,
  to garnish

Heat the oil and butter in a saucepan over a medium–low heat. Add the garlic and red pepper. Cook for a few seconds until the garlic is just beginning to colour. Stir in the tomato purée and wine. Cook for 10 minutes, stirring.

Bring a large saucepan of lightly salted water to the boil. Add the pasta, bring back to the boil and cook for 8–10 minutes, or until tender but still firm to the bite. Drain and return to the pan.

Add the prawns to the sauce and increase the heat to medium–high. Cook for 2 minutes, stirring, until the prawns turn pink. Reduce the heat and stir in the cream. Cook for 1 minute, stirring constantly, until thickened. Season with salt and pepper.

Transfer the pasta to a warmed serving dish. Pour the sauce over the pasta. Sprinkle with the parsley. Toss well to mix and serve at once.

Fusilli with
Monkfish & Broccoli

SERVES 4

115 g/4 oz broccoli, divided into florets

3 tbsp olive oil

350 g/12 oz monkfish fillet, skinned
   and cut into bite-sized pieces

2 garlic cloves, crushed

125 ml/4 fl oz dry white wine

225 ml/8 fl oz double cream

400 g/14 oz dried fusilli

85 g/3 oz Gorgonzola cheese, diced

salt and pepper

Divide the broccoli florets into tiny sprigs. Bring a saucepan of lightly salted water to the boil, add the broccoli and cook for 2 minutes. Drain and refresh under cold running water.

Heat the oil in a large, heavy-based frying pan. Add the monkfish and garlic and season to taste with salt and pepper. Cook, stirring frequently, for 5 minutes, or until the fish is opaque. Pour in the white wine and cream and cook, stirring occasionally, for 5 minutes, or until the fish is cooked through and the sauce has thickened. Stir in the broccoli florets.

Bring a large saucepan of lightly salted water to the boil. Add the pasta, bring back to the boil and cook for 8-10 minutes, until the pasta is tender but still firm to the bite. Drain and tip the pasta into the pan with the fish, add the cheese and toss lightly. Serve immediately.

Penne with
Squid & Tomatoes

SERVES 4

225 g/8 oz dried penne

350 g/12 oz prepared squid

6 tbsp olive oil

2 onions, sliced

225 ml/8 fl oz fish or chicken stock

150 ml/5 fl oz full-bodied red wine

400 g/14 oz canned chopped
   tomatoes

2 tbsp tomato purée

1 tbsp chopped fresh marjoram

1 bay leaf

salt and pepper

2 tbsp chopped fresh parsley,
   to garnish

Bring a large saucepan of lightly salted water to the boil. Add the pasta, bring back to the boil and cook for 8-10 minutes, until the pasta is tender but still firm to the bite. With a sharp knife, cut the squid into strips.

Heat the oil in a large saucepan. Add the onions and cook over a low heat, stirring occasionally, for 5 minutes, or until soft. Add the squid and fish stock, bring to the boil and simmer for 3 minutes. Stir in the wine, chopped tomatoes and their can juices, tomato purée, marjoram and bay leaf. Season to taste with salt and pepper. Bring to the boil and cook for 5 minutes, or until slightly reduced.

Add the pasta, return to the boil and simmer for 5–7 minutes, or until tender but still firm to the bite. Remove and discard the bay leaf. Transfer to a warmed serving dish, garnish with the parsley and serve immediately.

Linguine
with Mixed Seafood

SERVES 4–6

2 tbsp olive oil

2 shallots, finely chopped

2 garlic cloves, finely chopped

1 small red chilli, deseeded and finely
  chopped

200 g/7 oz canned chopped
  tomatoes

½ bunch fresh flat-leaf parsley,
  chopped, plus extra sprigs
  to garnish

pinch of sugar

450 g/1 lb live mussels

450 g/1 lb live clams

6 tbsp dry white wine

1 lemon, sliced

175 g/6 oz large cooked prawns,
  peeled and deveined

450 g/1 lb linguine

salt and pepper

Heat the oil in a saucepan. Add the shallots, garlic and chilli and cook over a low heat, stirring occasionally, for 5 minutes. Increase the heat to medium, stir in the tomatoes and their can juices, parsley and sugar and season to taste with salt and pepper. Bring to the boil, then cover and simmer, stirring occasionally, for 15–20 minutes. Scrub the mussels and clams under cold running water and pull off the 'beards' from the mussels. Discard any with broken shells or any that refuse to close when tapped.

Pour the wine into a large saucepan with a tight-fitting lid and add the lemon slices, mussels and clams. Cover and cook over a high heat, shaking the pan occasionally, for 5 minutes, until all the shellfish have opened. Using a slotted spoon, transfer the shellfish to a bowl and reserve the cooking liquid. Discard any mussels and clams that remain closed. Reserve a few for the garnish and remove the remainder from their shells. Strain the cooking liquid through a muslin-lined sieve.

Bring a large saucepan of lightly salted water to the boil. Add the pasta, bring back to the boil and cook for 8–10 minutes, until tender but still firm to the bite. Meanwhile, stir the strained cooking liquid into the shallot and tomato mixture and bring to the boil, stirring constantly. Add the shelled mussels and clams and the prawns. Taste and adjust the seasoning, if necessary, and heat through gently. Drain the pasta and return it to the pan. Add the shellfish mixture and toss well. Divide among individual warmed plates, garnish with the reserved mussels and clams and garnish with parsley and serve.

vegetarian

Fettuccine
all'Alfredo

SERVES 4

2 tbsp butter

200 ml/7 fl oz double cream

450 g/1 lb dried fettuccine

85 g/3 oz freshly grated Parmesan
  cheese, plus extra to serve

pinch of freshly grated nutmeg

salt and pepper

1 fresh flat-leaf parsley sprig,
  to garnish

Put the butter and 150 ml/5 fl oz of the cream into a large saucepan and bring the mixture to the boil over a medium heat. Reduce the heat, then simmer gently for 1½ minutes, or until the cream has thickened slightly.

Bring a large saucepan of lightly salted water to the boil. Add the pasta, bring back to the boil and cook for 8-10 minutes, until the pasta is tender but still firm to the bite. Drain thoroughly and return to the pan, then pour over the cream sauce.

Toss the pasta in the sauce over a low heat, stirring with a wooden spoon, until coated thoroughly.

Add the remaining cream, Parmesan cheese and nutmeg to the pasta mixture and season to taste with salt and pepper. Toss the pasta in the mixture while heating through.

Transfer the pasta mixture to a warmed serving plate and garnish with the fresh parsley sprig. Serve immediately with grated Parmesan cheese.

Spaghettini
with Tomatoes & Black Olives

SERVES 4

1 tbsp olive oil

1 garlic clove, finely chopped

2 tsp bottled capers, drained, rinsed
and chopped

12 black olives, stoned and chopped

½ dried red chilli, crushed

1¼ kg/2 lb 12 oz canned tomatoes

1 tbsp chopped fresh parsley,
plus extra to garnish

350 g/12 oz dried spaghettini

salt

2 tbsp freshly grated Parmesan
cheese , to serve

Heat the oil in a large, heavy-based frying pan. Add the garlic and cook over a low heat for 30 seconds, then add the capers, olives, dried chilli, tomatoes and their can juices, season to taste with salt. Partially cover the pan and simmer gently for 20 minutes.

Stir in the parsley, partially cover the frying pan again and simmer for a further 10 minutes.

Bring a large saucepan of lightly salted water to the boil. Add the pasta, bring back to the boil and cook for 8-10 minutes, until the pasta is tender but still firm to the bite. Drain and transfer to a warmed serving dish. Add the sauce and toss well. Sprinkle the Parmesan cheese over the pasta and garnish with extra chopped parsley. Serve immediately.

Olive, Pepper &
Cherry Tomato Pasta

SERVES 4

225 g/8 oz dried penne

2 tbsp olive oil

25 g/1 oz butter

2 garlic cloves, crushed

1 green pepper, deseeded and thinly
   sliced

1 yellow pepper, deseeded and thinly
   sliced

16 cherry tomatoes, halved

1 tbsp chopped fresh oregano,
   plus extra sprigs to garnish

125 ml/4 fl oz dry white wine

2 tbsp quartered, stoned black
   olives

75 g/2¾ oz rocket

salt and pepper

Bring a large saucepan of lightly salted water to the boil. Add the pasta, bring back to the boil and cook for 8-10 minutes, until the pasta is tender but still firm to the bite. Drain the pasta thoroughly.

Heat the oil and butter in a frying pan until the butter melts. Sauté the garlic for 30 seconds. Add the peppers and cook, stirring constantly, for 3–4 minutes.

Stir in the cherry tomatoes, oregano, wine and olives and cook for 3–4 minutes. Season well with salt and pepper and stir in the rocket until just wilted. Transfer the pasta to a serving dish, spoon over the sauce and garnish with oregano sprigs. Serve immediately.

Rigatoni
with Gorgonzola Sauce

SERVES 4

400 g/14 oz dried rigatoni
25 g/1 oz unsalted butter
6 fresh sage leaves
200 g/7 oz Gorgonzola cheese, diced
175–225 ml/6–8 fl oz double cream
2 tbsp dry vermouth
salt and pepper

Bring a large saucepan of lightly salted water to the boil. Add the pasta, bring back to the boil and cook for 8-10 minutes, until the pasta is tender but still firm to the bite.

Meanwhile, melt the butter in a heavy-based saucepan. Add the sage leaves and cook, stirring gently, for 1 minute. Remove and reserve the sage leaves. Add the cheese and cook over a low heat, stirring constantly, until it has melted. Gradually, stir in 175 ml/6 fl oz of the cream and the vermouth. Season to taste with salt and pepper and cook, stirring, until thickened. Add more cream if the sauce seems too thick.

Drain the pasta well and transfer to a warmed serving dish. Add the sauce, toss well to mix and serve immediately, garnished with the reserved sage leaves.

Rigatoni
with Peppers & Goat's Cheese

SERVES 4

2 tbsp olive oil

1 tbsp butter

1 small onion, finely chopped

4 peppers, yellow and red, deseeded
    and cut into 2-cm/3/4-inch squares

3 garlic cloves, thinly sliced

450 g/1 lb dried rigatoni

125 g/4½ oz goat's cheese, crumbled

15 fresh basil leaves, shredded

10 black olives, stoned and sliced

salt and pepper

Heat the oil and butter in a large frying pan over a medium heat. Add the onion and cook until soft. Increase the heat to medium–high and add the peppers and garlic. Cook for 12–15 minutes, stirring, until the peppers are tender but not mushy. Season to taste with salt and pepper. Remove from the heat.

Bring a large saucepan of lightly salted water to the boil. Add the pasta, bring back to the boil and cook for 8–10 minutes, or until tender but still firm to the bite. Drain and transfer to a warmed serving dish. Add the cheese and toss to mix.

Briefly reheat the sauce. Add the basil and olives. Pour over the pasta and toss well to mix. Serve immediately.

Linguine
with *Wild Mushrooms*

SERVES 4

55 g/2 oz butter

1 onion, chopped

1 garlic clove, finely chopped

350 g/12 oz wild mushrooms, sliced

350 g/12 oz dried linguine

300 ml/10 fl oz crème fraîche

2 tbsp shredded fresh basil leaves,
   plus extra to garnish

4 tbsp freshly grated Parmesan
   cheese, plus extra to serve

salt and pepper

Melt the butter in a large, heavy-based frying pan. Add the onion and garlic and cook over a low heat for 5 minutes, or until soft. Add the mushrooms and cook, stirring occasionally, for a further 10 minutes.

Meanwhile, bring a large, saucepan of lightly salted water to the boil. Add the pasta, return to the boil and cook for 8–10 minutes, or until tender but still firm to the bite.

Stir the crème fraîche, basil and Parmesan cheese into the mushroom mixture and season to taste with salt and pepper. Cover and heat through gently for 1–2 minutes. Drain the pasta and transfer to a warmed serving dish. Add the mushroom mixture and toss lightly. Garnish with extra basil and serve immediately with extra Parmesan cheese.

Linguine
with Roasted Garlic & Red Peppers

SERVES 4

6 large garlic cloves, unpeeled

400 g/14 oz bottled roasted red
   peppers, drained and sliced

200 g/7 oz canned chopped
   tomatoes

3 tbsp olive oil

¼ tsp dried chilli flakes

1 tsp chopped fresh thyme or
   oregano

350 g/12 oz dried linguine

salt and pepper

Place the unpeeled garlic cloves in a shallow, ovenproof dish. Roast in a preheated oven at 200°C/400°F/Gas Mark 6 for 7–10 minutes, until the cloves feel soft.

Put the peppers, tomatoes and their can juices, and oil in a food processor or blender, then purée. Squeeze the garlic flesh into the purée. Add the chilli flakes and thyme. Season to taste with salt and pepper. Blend again, then scrape into a saucepan and set aside.

Bring a large saucepan of lightly salted water to the boil. Add the pasta, bring back to the boil and cook for 8–10 minutes, or until tender but still firm to the bite. Drain and transfer to a warmed serving dish.

Reheat the sauce and pour over the pasta. Toss well to mix and serve immediately.

Pasta
with Green Vegetables

SERVES 4

225 g/8 oz dried fusilli

1 head green broccoli, cut into florets

2 courgettes, sliced

225 g/8 oz asparagus spears,
   trimmed

125 g/4½ oz mangetout

125 g/4½ oz frozen peas

25 g/1 oz butter

3 tbsp vegetable stock

5 tbsp double cream

large pinch of freshly grated nutmeg

salt and pepper

2 tbsp chopped fresh parsley and
   2 tbsp freshly grated Parmesan
   cheese, to serve

Bring a large, saucepan of lightly salted water to the boil. Add the pasta, return to the boil and cook for 8–10 minutes, or until tender but still firm to the bite. Drain the pasta in a colander, return to the pan, cover and keep warm.

Steam the broccoli, courgettes, asparagus spears and mangetout over a saucepan of boiling, salted water until just beginning to soften. Remove from the heat and plunge into cold water to prevent further cooking. Drain and reserve. Cook the peas in boiling, salted water for 3 minutes, then drain. Refresh in cold water and drain again.

Place the butter and stock in a saucepan over a medium heat. Add all the vegetables except for the asparagus spears and toss carefully with a wooden spoon to heat through, taking care not to break them up. Stir in the cream, allow the sauce to heat through and season to taste with salt, pepper and nutmeg.

Transfer the pasta to a warmed serving dish and stir in the chopped parsley. Spoon the sauce over and arrange the asparagus spears on top. Sprinkle with the freshly grated Parmesan cheese and serve hot.